Volunteering

Other titles in the series Life—A How-to Guide

Dealing With Stress
A How-to Guide
Library ed. 978-0-7660-3439-6
Paperback 978-1-59845-309-6

Choosing a Community Service Career
A How-to Guide
Library ed. 978-1-59845-147-4
Paperback 978-1-59845-312-6

Friendship
A How-to Guide
Library ed. 978-0-7660-3442-6
Paperback 978-1-59845-315-7

Getting Ready to Drive
A How-to Guide
Library ed. 978-0-7660-3443-3
Paperback 978-1-59845-314-0

Getting the Hang of Fashion and Dress Codes
A How-to Guide
Library ed. 978-0-7660-3444-0
Paperback 978-1-59845-313-3

Using Technology
A How-to Guide
Library ed. 978-0-7660-3441-9
Paperback 978-1-59845-311-9

Volunteering

A How-to Guide

Life
A
How-to
Guide

Audrey Borus

DONATION BOX

E Enslow Publishers, Inc.
40 Industrial Road
Box 398
Berkeley Heights, NJ 07922
USA

http://www.enslow.com

Acknowledgments

Special thanks to the Education Development Center, Newton, Massachusetts, and particularly to Leslie Hergert and Wendy Rivenburgh for graciously answering questions and pointing me in the right direction; to all the youth organizers who took the time to answer me; and to Signe: you can change the world.

Library of Congress Cataloging-in-Publication Data

Borus, Audrey.
  Volunteering : a how-to guide / Audrey Borus.
    p. cm.—(Life—a how-to guide)
  Includes bibliographical references and index.
  Summary: "Learn about different kinds of volunteering, reasons why people volunteer, and organizations that you can join to get involved"—Provided by publisher.
  ISBN 978-0-7660-3440-2
  1. Young volunteers—Juvenile literature. 2. Voluntarism—Juvenile literature. I. Title.
  HN49.V64B678 2011
  302'.14—dc22

                            2010029586

Paperback ISBN: 978-1-59845-310-2

Printed in the United States of America

072011 Lake Book Manufacturing, Inc., Melrose Park, IL

10 9 8 7 6 5 4 3 2 1

To Our Readers: We have done our best to make sure all Internet addresses in this book were active and appropriate when we went to press. However, the author and the publisher have no control over and assume no liability for the material available on those Internet sites or on other Web sites they may link to. Any comments or suggestions can be sent by e-mail to comments@enslow.com or to the address on the back cover.

♻ Enslow Publishers, Inc., is committed to printing our books on recycled paper. The paper in every book contains 10% to 30% post-consumer waste (PCW). The cover board on the outside of each book contains 100% PCW. Our goal is to do our part to help young people and the environment too!

Illustration Credits: All clipart © 2011 Clipart.com, a division of Getty Images. All rights reserved.; AP Images/David Brock, p. 85; AP Images/George Osodi, p. 34; AP Images/Gunnar Ask, p. 39; AP Images/Leandro Huebner, p. 103; AP Images/Paul Sakuma, p. 16; AP Images/Peter DiCampo, p. 31; AP Images/Salva Dut, p. 20; AP Images/Thomas Wright, p. 64; AP Images/Tom Hanson, p. 41; AP Images/T. Rob Brown, p. 104; © Bryngelzon/iStockphoto.com, p. 67; Courtesy Always Ready Kids, p. 82; Courtesy American Red Cross Bay Area Chapter, p. 28; Courtesy of Littleneck-Douglaston Community Ambulance, p. 76; © dlewis33/iStockphoto.com, p. 45; © ImageegamI/iStockphoto.com, p. 56; © Jani Bryson/iStockphoto, p. 1; © Lori Martin/Shutterstock.com, p. 74; © LynnSeeden/iStockphoto.com, p. 48; © Make the Road New York, p. 106; © Megan Nakahara, pp. 24, 25; © MoniqueRodriguez/iStockphoto.com, p. 22; © 2011 Photos.com, a division of Getty Images. All rights reserved., pp. 42, 73, 87, 88; © Ralph125/iStockphoto.com, p. 11; © Richard Curtain, p. 62; Shutterstock.com, pp. 3, 9, 14, 18, 51, 53, 58, 61, 92, 96; © The Revolving Museum, p. 79.

Cover Credit: Shutterstock.com (female volunteer).

Contents

Chapter 1

Who, Me?

Opportunities to improve your community are all around you. If you want to make a positive change, you may find opportunities for community service in the most unlikely places. Take for example, the kids at the 4-H Model Horse Club in Salmon, Idaho. Their interest in horses led them to a community service project helping horses on Turtle Bay Island in the Bahamas.

The Model Horse Club's story actually starts centuries before, when Christopher Columbus first landed in the New World. In addition to everything else, he brought horses with him that could help in exploration and colonization.

Today, eight special horses, descendants of the Spanish horses who first traveled to the Americas in the 1400s, live on a tiny strip of land called Turtle Bay Island. It is one of the seven hundred islands that make up the Bahamas. Historians and horse buffs believe they are there because the Caribbean was an important place for these Spanish travelers. They set up breeding stations for their horses and exported them to the colonies in North and South America. In the process, many ships transporting the horses were wrecked on the islands of the Caribbean. Today's horses are called the Abaco Barbs, and they are believed to be the descendants of a herd that once may have numbered two hundred. They represent a marvel of nature: transcending time, the elements, and the creep of development.

When Susan Dudasik told the kids from the Salmon Model Horse Club that these horses were near extinction, the kids knew they wanted to do something. But their first thought was, "What can we do? We're only kids." Cameron Angeny, one of the kids in the group, said:

> The club didn't really need to be convinced to
> do something. I guess due to Susan's
> enthusiasm we all wanted to help the horses.
> I had read a book named *Jingo: Wild Horse of
> Abaco* by Jocelyn Arundel. My Mom and I
> were discussing what we could possibly do for
> the horses, and she mentioned getting a
> Breyer model of Misty and the book *Misty of
> Chincoteague* when she was little. I wondered

if I could get Breyer involved somehow and get them to sell Jingo and an Abaco Barb model and donate part of the proceeds to the Abaco Barb horses.[1]

Cameron brought the idea to the club. The kids brainstormed and developed a plan. They petitioned Breyer Animal Creations about developing a model Abaco Barb horse that would help raise awareness about them. Breyer was impressed. The company created the new line in 2005 and donated a portion of their profits to Arkwild, an organization dedicated to preserving the horses.

Cameron says he learned a lot from this project. For example, he says, "Not all endangered species are starving, or have the same problems as one another."[2] He also learned that there are sides to every issue. In the case of the Abaco Barb, citrus farmers on the island have turned the forest into groves, using chemicals to treat their crops, such as fertilizers, pesticides, and herbicides. But the heavy use of chemicals produces overly rich grazing material for the horses, which veterinarians believe causes them to get fat and lame. "The farmers are just trying to make a living and keep their families fed. They didn't start out intending to harm these horses. The horses have been running free for a long time and they're not used to having fences and a change in their environment."[3]

Today, in spite of some setbacks—such as fires and drought in May 2010—new forage for the horses is slowly growing and more areas in which they can roam have been fenced.

The 4-H Model Horse Club in Salmon, Idaho, volunteered their efforts to support a group of endangered horses.

Asked whether he had advice for young volunteers like himself, Cameron answered:

> You can make a difference in the world. You don't have to go overseas to make a difference; you can do it from home. I would encourage young people to try and make a difference and improve the world. We need to be aware of our environment. I'm not saying we shouldn't build houses or anything, but I think it's good to be aware. Make sure that you aren't deliberately, or unnecessarily, harming the environment. It is a balance, and the environment is going to have to change as a result of people just living and progressing. But don't be afraid of trying to make a difference![4]

What Is Volunteering?

So what exactly is volunteering? All definitions of volunteering include the following four elements:

1. Volunteering is voluntary; you do it because you choose to.
2. You don't get a financial reward for volunteering; essentially, you donate your time and talents.
3. You perform your volunteer work through a formal arrangement (such as with a nonprofit organization, a

A teen volunteer saws planks for a boardwalk in a wildlife park in Blue Springs State Park, Florida. Nearly 16 million kids under age eighteen are volunteers.

Who, Me?

government agency, a school, or a business) or through an informal arrangement, such as helping neighbors or friends.

4. Your volunteering benefits others: people in need, your community, and even you.

Volunteering is a helpful activity. By helping someone less fortunate, you may feel better about your life. It may also move you to consider a variety of other ways that you can help others. True volunteering is something you plan to do, maybe even before someone asks you to. And it requires some commitment of your time and your energy.

Volunteering in the United States and Abroad

Right now in the United States, about 26 percent of the population is under age eighteen—that is about 70 million people. About 15.5 million kids under eighteen are youth volunteers. They are people like you, who spend money, have thoughts and opinions, and care about things. In the United States, a typical youth volunteer contributes about twenty-nine hours per year.[5] That may not sound like a whole lot for the time span of an entire year, but these young people are making many significant contributions to their communities.

All kinds of organizations offer opportunities for you to volunteer. In fact, you may already know about some of them through your school. Or you may be required to take a course in which you spend some time providing a service to your community (such as visiting residents at a nursing home) and some of your time in class evaluating your volunteer experience. The latter is called service learning, and while volunteering is a major part of it, identifying the new skills and knowledge that you are gaining is also important. Through service learning, you learn about an issue or problem, figure out an appropriate action, then apply your skills to help solve that problem. For example, if you volunteer at a homeless shelter, you may go back to class to learn about the issues surrounding homelessness and its causes. You could also look at what some U.S. cities are doing to help the homeless. This process allows students to practice their communication skills by learning how to explain the problem and learning how to communicate with the people they are helping.

Another type of volunteering is available through youth leadership organizations, such as 4-H, Boy Scouts, or Girl Scouts. These organizations emphasize volunteering, rather than formal learning. But that is not to say you won't be learning anything, it's just that there are most likely no specific learning objectives as there are in a class. For example, depending on your individual experience, volunteering may help you develop leadership skills or teach you how to think more broadly about a community issue.

4-H Hot Shots

Kids in the 4-H club in Poughkeepsie, New York, created, bottled, and sold a half ton of Hot Shot Nectarine Salsa, their own unique creation. The kids were involved in the whole process. First, they researched the food business. Then they worked with a chef to create a recipe, testing it at the local farmers' market. They also worked with Food Tech, a business whose specialty is food products. Through Food Tech, they learned about Food and Drug Administration (FDA) regulations. They also got tips on designing their product's packaging.

The teens grew fresh fruits and vegetables for their salsa with seeds they cultivated to thrive in Poughkeepsie's climate. They didn't have a lot of room, either, since their center is downtown. But they were able to prepare, process, and cook enough salsa to bottle 1,300 jars. They sold 80 percent of their stock within the first month of business.

So what did they learn?

"I've learned how to be more conscious about the things that I do and decisions that I make, and I've learned that hard work builds character," said Paris Sims, one of the club members. Another member, Barbara Belotte, said she learned to budget and keep track of money, as well as the time and patience that it takes to make a business a success. And now, the kids are learning something else: Hot Shot Salsa was so popular that they ran out. The kids are experimenting with ways to change their business plan to meet the demand for their product.[6]

The 4-H Club members grew their own produce for their salsa.

All over the world, there are organizations that raise awareness about volunteerism and provide the technical assistance to help volunteers organize. It is hard to pinpoint just how many young volunteers there are worldwide, but with many young people eager to help their communities, many organizations around the world are looking for ways to involve young people. One of the biggest organizations is United Nations Volunteers (UNV). UNV is based in Bonn, Germany, and it is active in more than 140 countries.

Why Volunteer?

Whether you volunteer through your school or another organization, you are very likely to benefit from the experience. Volunteering is a rewarding experience, and it may help you decide what you want to do later in life. You'll get to help people who really need it.

Volunteering benefits you and your community. For you, some benefits include:

A sense of self-worth. Everyone knows that when you do something good, you feel good. Many experts say that the cornerstone of respect is self-respect. You have probably heard it said more than once that it is easier to respect others if you first respect yourself. And what is self-respect? It is your ability to recognize your strengths and weaknesses and to take care of your mind and your body by trying to eat well, exercise regularly, and get enough sleep.

Take the girls of the Allegheny County Girls as Grantmakers (ACGAG) in Pennsylvania. This group opposed a line of T-shirts that clothing retailer Abercrombie & Fitch was selling. The tees had slogans printed across them—phrases such as "I had a nightmare I was a brunette" and "I hope you can make more

Like the Allegheny County Girls as Grantmakers, this group objects to stereotyped messages on Abercrombie & Fitch T-shirts and is calling for a boycott of the store.

than I can spend"—lines the girls felt were offensive not just to them but to all girls and women. So they organized a boycott. "It's important," said one of the group's members, "that young women must not think 'it's OK to see us for bodies, not our minds.'" Sixteen-year-old Emma Blackman-Mathis, cochair of the group, told reporters, "We're telling [girls] to think about the fact that they're being degraded. We're all going to come together in this one effort to fight the message that we're getting from pop culture."[7]

While many adults were sympathetic, few thought the girls could actually persuade Abercrombie & Fitch to remove the shirts. This wasn't the first time the company had been under fire for its racist and sexist marketing. But the organizers of ACGAG met with Abercrombie & Finch executives armed with some T-shirt suggestions of their own. In the end, shirts were pulled from stores. Though Abercrombie & Fitch didn't take any of the girls' suggestions, they did tone down the slogans on their tees.

Fifteen-year-old Emily McGinty reflects that her group never expected to get as far as they did. Voicing an opinion shared by many of the girls who were involved, she said, "This whole thing has just given me so much confidence. This has taught us that everyone has a chance to be heard, and that even a whisper is something to break the silence."[8]

Fighting the Cold in Argentina

Ruca Antu School is located in Junin de los Andes, a poor town in Southern Argentina. Though there are beautiful mountains, the winters can be quite cold. Every winter people in Junin de los Andes are confronted with the lack of heating resources. But in 1999, the students at this school began thinking of ways to beat the cold. Their teacher, Professor Rosa Maria Teti, explained that during World War II, Italians suffered through winters without firewood. She told them that people would take any scraps of paper they could find, wet them, then dry them into briquettes. There is no shortage of scraps in Junin de los Andes, and the students began thinking that this might be a solution to their problem. They did some research and some testing. Using a press built by kids at the provincial technical high school, Ruca Antu students pressed scraps of paper into tightly compacted logs they called Ecoleños (*leños* means logs in Spanish). Within a few hours of burning the logs in a stove, a room that had been 62 degrees Fahrenheit was warmed to almost 70. They could use the logs to boil water. In 2000, they improved their methods, finding just the right combination of chopped paper, dried leaves, sawdust chips, and potato peels to make a burnable mix. "For the students, it was an extraordinary experience," said one teacher. "They've learned a lot about scientific method."[9] This is all the more remarkable when you consider that most of the kids at Ruca Antu have disabilities, many of which have been caused by malnutrition and parental alcoholism.

This story illustrates an activity closely related to volunteering: activism. Activism encompasses a range of activities. But, the point of activism is to provide a framework for changing things, define areas for engaging, and motivating people to act. Activism often depends on volunteers.

A sense of empowerment. Along with a sense of self-worth, another positive effect of volunteering is the feeling that you can make a difference. You see something wrong in your community, set about changing it, and get it done. You also get a chance to develop skills, such as organizing a meeting or polling people for their opinion. You get to share your point of view about things that are important to you.

Consider the case of Ryan Hrelijac. When he was six years old, Ryan learned that clean water is critical to good health, but many people around the world do not have access to clean water. Ryan decided to raise money for people who didn't have clean water. For four months, he did household chores to raise seventy dollars. While his older brothers played, Ryan cleaned. To encourage him, his mom drew a red thermometer on a piece of paper with thirty-five lines across it, each line representing two dollars. For every two dollars he earned, Ryan filled in a line. He put his earnings into an old cookie tin.

When Ryan's grandfather got wind of the project, he hired Ryan and his brothers to pick up pinecones. They earned ten dollars for each garbage bag they filled. Ryan's parents gave him another five dollars for a good report card. All the money went into his tin as the thermometer got closer to being fully colored.

A young boy drinks water from a well in Sudan, Africa. Many people around the world do not have access to clean water.

When Ryan got close to reaching his goal, his mom wondered, "Where do you donate seventy dollars?" A friend who worked at an international development organization told them about a small nonprofit agency in Ottawa, Canada, called WaterCan that builds wells in developing countries. The friend arranged for Ryan to give WaterCan the money in person.

On the day of their meeting, Ryan handed over his cookie tin to then executive director Nicole Bosley. He added an extra five dollars saying, "You might want to feed the people making the well." Bosley thanked him and told him about WaterCan's clean-water projects. She said that while seventy dollars would buy a hand pump, it would cost closer to two thousand to drill a well, to which Ryan replied, "I'll just do more chores, then."

The Canadian International Development Agency (CIDA) matches WaterCan's funds two for one, so Ryan would need almost seven hundred dollars to build his well. Ryan's parents weren't sure what to do. They recognized his hard work, but felt his goal was not achievable. But the next week, the friend who had put them in touch with WaterCan e-mailed her family and friends about Ryan's project. They donated enough money to dig Ryan's well. The first well was built in 1999, when Ryan was seven years old, for a school in Uganda. That well continues to serve thousands of people. Meanwhile, Ryan's

determination grew into a foundation that is a recognized nonprofit organization, contributing a total of more than six hundred wells and bringing clean water and sanitation services to many countries throughout the world.[10]

A teenager helps out at an animal hospital. All kinds of organizations offer volunteer opportunities.

Think about Ryan and the girls in Allegheny. Though they used different tools—the girls used boycotting and Ryan used fund-raising—their results were similar. Both activities brought about important changes in their communities.

A sense of belonging. Being a good citizen is important to having involvement in your community. But what exactly does it really mean? Could good citizenship mean picking up after yourself? Doing what you know is right, even when there is no one watching? If you answered yes to these questions, you'd be right. But there's more.

Citizenship also refers to your responsibility toward, or contribution to, your community as well as your conduct within your community and nation. Citzenship is not just a legal concept. According to Ruth Lister, Professor of Social Policy at Loughborough University, England, citizenship is "about membership in a community and the rights and obligations that flow from that membership."[11] It means you follow the rules and participate in making them. It means that you speak out for what you believe in. It can also mean that you volunteer at your local soup kitchen. Or it might mean that you work with your local animal shelter to find homes for abandoned pets.

Some people believe that because volunteering is an expression of citizenship, it is a critical component of a democracy.[12] When you participate by helping people, by speaking out about what you think is wrong or what could be improved, you are involved.

Recognizing involvement is the aim of the Prudential Spirit of Community Awards. Each year, this organization, along with the National Association of Secondary School Principals, selects two students from every state (one in high school and one in middle school) to acknowledge their outstanding volunteer service to their communities. The honorees receive $1,000 awards, engraved silver medallions, and an all-expense-paid trip to Washington, D.C., for four days of sharing their experiences, learning about community service, and recognition.

Megan Nakahara, known as Meimei, volunteered to help Hawaiian green sea turtles.

Volunteering

Megan Nakahara, a middle-school student from Hawaii, wasn't thinking about awards when she volunteered to help Hawaiian green sea turtles, a species that live in the waters around the island of Hawaii. The turtles are endangered because commercial turtle hunters used to catch them for local restaurants.

Meimei (as her friends and family call her) attended the Hawai'i Preparatory Academy. Her interest in turtles started when she was in fourth grade.

Her class went on an excursion to work with the Sea Turtle Research Program, a collaboration between her school and the Marine Turtle Research Program. Right away, Meimei knew she wanted to be involved. "I really enjoyed it and that was my inspiration in wanting to help out. When I was given the opportunity to help the Hawaiian green sea turtle, *Chelonia mydas,* at one of our school's study sites at the Mauna Lani Bay Hotel and Resort, I was very excited." Meimei was awarded a Prudential Spirit of Community Award for her critical role in a project that monitors the turtles and informs the public about their plight. First, Meimei learned as much as she could about the turtles so she could help educate the public.

Soon, she was going on regular data-collection trips, where she carefully measured turtles' width, length, thickness, and weight so their growth could be tracked over time.

These days, Meimei thinks she wants to be a marine scientist. "I learned so much about the Hawaiian green sea turtle, data collection, and how to work as part of a team. I have memories of the turtles and what they would do from each trip. . . . I always looked forward to going on these trips because they are enjoyable! I will never forget that volunteering can be fun, even if you have to work hard."[13]

Improved well-being. Studies show that the more social ties you have, the better you feel, especially as you get older. Volunteering is a way for people to get involved in their communities. And it comes with the added benefit of helping you feel better, both physically and mentally. In fact, some experts believe that if you continue to volunteer into your old age, you'll live longer.[14]

New skills and knowledge. As a volunteer, you can develop your civic skills, such as the ability to organize a meeting, speak in front of groups, and write a convincing letter. Or you might even learn how to run a business. Volunteering also allows you to meet people who are doing jobs that you might like to do one day. And even more importantly, volunteering can give you a whole different perspective on the world around you.

Of course, volunteering isn't just about what you get out of it. Your volunteer work also does something for your community and the people in it.

Helping people in need. Through volunteering, you help people who might not otherwise be helped: an elderly acquaintance, a homeless person, or someone with a physical disability. For example, the Youth for Chinese Elderly (YCE) program in San Francisco, an initiative of the Bay Area Red Cross, trains young volunteers to help their elders prepare for disaster. On Saturday mornings, volunteers travel to senior buildings to teach elderly Chinese about disaster preparedness. There are five hundred youth volunteers spread throughout nine different San Francisco high schools. Kayi Lau is one of the members of the YCE at Lincoln High School, not far from Golden Gate Park. She started volunteering with friends and then became the club's president. Kayi says:

> In my opinion, all of us who volunteer feel as though it's an important part of our lives—especially as we are part of the Chinese-American community here. We all feel passionate about teaching people how to help save lives. First, I was an officer and helped organize and run a club of fifty people. It was hard, but I learned a lot more than I expected. I am now experienced as a leader and can make responsible decisions. Additionally, I've improved my communication skills with all kinds of people. From being a leader with the American Red Cross, I have learned how to speak up when needed and solve problems

Members of the Lincoln High School Youth for Chinese Elderly (YCE) program in San Francisco.

maturely. Working with the elderly has given me the opportunity to do something I enjoy while giving back to my community. I've also discovered that volunteering filled an emptiness in me and has made my life more meaningful. My desire to continue volunteering is made even stronger by the smiles of those whom I have helped along the way. Through these activities with the elderly, it feels as though I have helped close the generation gap—at least a little.[15]

YCE gives those who feel powerless a stronger sense of control over their lives.

Solving a specific problem. Raising funds for a new community center, beautifying an abandoned lot, or starting a food drive for people who are hungry—these are just some of the problems you might be able to solve through a community service project.

For Aislynn Rodeghiero, the problem was suburban families who were struggling to provide their families with basic necessities and had nowhere to turn for support. "I wanted to reach a mass of people who, given seeming affluence, have hidden (and not so hidden) needs," says Rodeghiero. She was often in Norwood, a town just outside Boston, and noticed what she calls "a landscape of need; individuals loitering in the town center, hanging out at the local coffee shop, folks walking with stuffed shopping carts around town, single mothers with children selling lemonade at the side street corner in order to earn money for new school clothes." Rodeghiero decided it was a community that could use an outreach program. "I spent many a day walking the streets of Norwood, saying hi to strangers as they milled around town, asking questions, desperately trying to understand their stories, learn of their needs and see what I could do to help them." What she learned was interesting: There was a common theme. Almost everyone she talked to seemed alone, disconnected from other human beings, while at the same time craving interaction. So she formed Abundant Table, a program offering hot meals to all. The organization strives to "dignify, respect, encourage, and edify all its guests." Rodeghiero acknowledges that it can be difficult to seek assistance from an organization, saying, "We try to make it as welcoming as we can. Instead of having to wait in line, visitors are served at the table, as a sign of respect. The personal touch makes the meal feel less like a handout, visitors say."[16]

Abundant Table eventually became a nonprofit organization with a board of directors. But Rodeghiero says there were many roadblocks along the way. "Despite our efforts to spread word of our program, we had only one person attend our first Wednesday night supper . . . Learning where to find the people who could use our program was a challenge but we smartened up over time. Word of mouth ended up being our best marketing tool. One person turned into ten, ten turned into thirty, and now in our seventh year of service, we are serving two meals a week in Norwood, welcoming over 200 individuals and families and have developed satellite sites in four other towns."[17]

When asked about her advice for anyone who wants to start this kind of program, Rodeghiero says: "My biggest advice is to always dream big and know that dreams can come true. But to make dreams a reality, the first step is to believe in yourself. Then find people who also believe in you and keep them close. . . . Never lose heart, keep pressing on, and acquire the money necessary to reach your goal. Never sell yourself short or avoid doing something out of fear."[18]

A sixth-grade boy in New Hampshire helps out at a soup kitchen and shelter.

A Legacy of Volunteering

In 1961, when John F. Kennedy was sworn in as the thirty-fifth president of the United States, he delivered a famous speech. It was short—only ten minutes. In it, Kennedy appealed to Americans to unite. He asked them to fight against tyranny, poverty, disease, and war itself. He concluded his speech with the words "Ask not what your country can do for you—ask what you can do for your country. My fellow citizens of the world, ask not what America will do for you, but what together we can do for the freedom of man." In this brief speech, Kennedy set forth the notion that service to community and country is a high honor indeed. It was later President Kennedy's idea to found the Peace Corps, where talented young men and women, would serve as "ambassadors of peace."[19] They travel to developing nations all around the world helping people build better communities through AIDS education, emerging technologies, and environmental preservation, among other services.

You may be thinking, "But I'm just one person. What can I do?" A small act can initiate a domino effect that ultimately makes a big impact. Whether you go out into your community and organize a service project, raise money to donate to a charitable organization, or write letters to promote awareness about an issue that is important to you, you are making a difference. Get your friends to come with you or join a group that's already tackling an issue that interests you. Whatever you decide, know that you can make a difference.

Around the World

Youth volunteers aren't unique to the United States. You can find examples of young people creating change all over the world.

Empowering youth in Nigeria. For as long as he can remember, Imoh Colins Edozie has worked to help young people. As a native Nigerian, Edozie realized some harsh truths about his country: "Nigeria is made up of about 250 ethnic groups and has a population of about 120 million people. The history of democratic rule and peaceful coexistence has been that of conflict, violence and coup d'etat."[20] Although a civilian government was elected in 1960, that government was overthrown in 1966 by a military coup. Since then, Nigeria has been ruled by series of military dictatorships. As Edozie says,

> Nigerian society has experienced a "might is right" attitude towards settling disputes and leadership. The various undemocratic political practices in Nigeria combined with the deterioration of traditional values and structure have created a situation in which the Nigerian people do not believe that democracy is possible, nor are they able to envision credible alternatives. There is a growing sense of disillusionment among the population along with a growing cycle of violence.

A slum area in Lagos, Nigeria. Imoh Colins Edozie wanted to help young people learn how to help improve conditions in their country.

34

Volunteering

According to Edozie, such hopelessness has led to ethnic and religious violence. He says: "Nigerians now see themselves as members of ethnic groups instead of citizens of a country."[21]

And what about young people? In a country where approximately 34 percent of the population is between the ages of ten and twenty-four and is expected to grow quickly,[22] Edozie worries that Nigerian youth have no experience of democracy. "They do not know what is expected of them, nor do they know what they can expect."[23] Edozie felt he had to create a program to educate students about their civic responsibility and give them the means to live peacefully. He also believed that it was critical to educate teachers on techniques for peace education and civic awareness:

> Knowledge is power. Part of the problem with our society is that young persons are not properly empowered to be agents of change. I felt that young people have the power to change their situation but they have to be motivated to take action. Students need to understand that they can be actors, not just spectators, and that their actions can effect more than just their immediate lives. If students can appreciate that they have the power to take charge of their destiny and change the situation around them, it will prevent fatalistic ideas that ordinary people have no power to change their situation.[24]

In 2005, Edozie traveled to Switzerland to make a presentation about his ideas. Many people were supportive of Edozie and his ideas and wanted to help him promote civic education in Nigeria. A couple attending Edozie's workshop believed that the project was important and that it could have a positive impact on Nigerian youth. They arranged a buffet dinner in support of Edozie. They invited friends and raised money to start an organization that would promote Edozie's ideas.

What started as an idea has now become an important peace organization. Thus in 2005, Protect Our Future Peace and Civic Education was born. It is a network of teachers and students who meet to exchange ideas and promote the best practices, all with the idea of promoting peaceful resolutions to conflicts and civic responsibility. Protect Our Future Peace and Civic Education has the support of the U.S. Institute of Peace.

The organization runs workshops for secondary-school teachers and selected students where they receive training on promoting peace and civic education in their schools and communities. They then share what they have learned with others at their schools. Each participating school forms a peace club that allows for further networking and peer mediation. The organization has published a manual detailing the rights and obligations of citizens, how fair elections should be conducted and monitored, and peace education. It explains how to promote a culture of peace in your community. As result, more students are being given the tools to widen their thinking.

About starting such an organization, Edozie says "the secret is to have faith, believe in yourself and keeping trying. Hard work does not kill, but it has its reward." Edozie acknowledges that it can be very difficult to start an organization like Protect Our Future Peace and Civic Education. But he encourages those who are interested in starting an organization to push through the difficult times and see their dream through to the end. "There will be times of countless frustration, there will be times when you will feel like giving up, but the truth is it is at those time that you are almost at your destination. It is at those times that you need to somehow find the strength and courage to move and get success."[25]

Fighting child labor in Pakistan. You might have heard the story of Iqbal Masih, the twelve-year-old Pakistani activist who spoke out against child labor in his country. Iqbal was forced to work in the hand-knotted carpet industry for most of his childhood. Iqbal's father had left his wife and family shortly after Iqbal was born. Iqbal's mother was unable to make enough money to support her family on her own. When he was four years old, Iqbal's mother needed money, so she sold his services for a sixteen-dollar advance.

This system of *peshgi* (loans) is not unusual in many countries. It is commonly called bonded labor, and it is considered a form of slavery. In bonded labor, a person is tricked or trapped into working for very little pay, usually as a way to repay a loan. Today, bonded labor is illegal in Pakistan.

Iqbal was required to work his first year as an apprentice. He was learning how to be a carpet weaver. He was not paid for this work because this work was considered training. But the cost of the food he ate and the tools he used were added to the original sixteen-dollar loan. When he made mistakes, he was fined, and more money was added to the loan.

The hours were long. Iqbal worked at least twelve hours a day, six days a week. The working conditions were awful. Iqbal and the other children squatted on a wooden bench and bent forward to tie millions of knots into carpets. Following a specific pattern, he carefully tied each knot.

The children were not allowed to speak. They had to work constantly. If they started to daydream, a guard would hit them. If they did not pay close attention to their work, they might cut their own hands with the sharp tools they used to cut the thread. Because the windows had to remain shut to protect the quality of the wool, the room where the kids worked was very hot. Only two lightbulbs dangled overhead.

If the children talked back, ran away, were homesick, or became physically sick, they were punished. Punishments could include severe beatings, being chained to a loom, extended periods of isolation in a dark closet, and being hung upside down. Iqbal often received punishments.

Iqbal worked in these conditions for six years. Meanwhile, his debt grew to $419. And his situation was not unique. Many children have worked under similar conditions. And many more continue to work in hopeless situations.

Iqbal Masih, who brought international attention to the horrors of child labor in Pakistan, was shot and killed in 1995 at the age of twelve.

39

But Iqbal Masih would not remain working in the carpet factory to repay his growing debt. Instead, Iqbal became an activist against child labor. Iqbal had heard about a meeting of the Bonded Labour Liberation Front (BLLF), an organization fighting the bonded labor system. One day after work, Iqbal snuck out to attend the meeting. There he learned that the Pakistani government had outlawed *peshgi*, or bonded labor, in 1992. In addition, the government had canceled all outstanding loans. After the meeting, Iqbal spoke with the president of the BLLF, Ehsan Ullah Khan. Khan helped Iqbal get the paperwork he needed to show his employer that he should be free. But Iqbal also wanted to free his fellow workers.

After leaving the carpet factory, Iqbal went to a BLLF school in Lahore. He began taking part in demonstrations and meetings to speak out against child labor. Once, he even pretended to be a worker so that he could question children about their work conditions. It was dangerous, but the information he gathered helped shut down the factory and free hundreds of children.

He began speaking at BLLF meetings and then to international activists and journalists about his life as a bonded-child laborer. Unintimidated and full of conviction, Iqbal captured the attention of many people, including the Reebok Human Rights Youth in Action Award Committee. In 1994, ABC News awarded him a Person of the Week award.

Six years as a bonded child affected Iqbal physically. At age ten, he was less than four feet tall and weighed only sixty pounds. He also suffered from kidney problems, a curved spine,

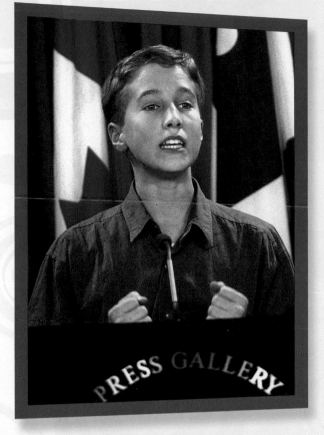

Craig Kielburger founded Free the Children in response to the death of Iqbal Masih.

bronchial infections, and arthritis. On Easter Sunday 1995, Iqbal was shot as he walked to his uncle's house. Though local criminals were charged, many believe that he was killed because of the negative publicity he brought to industries using child labor.

Iqbal's death inspired another youth activist, Craig Kielburger, a twelve-year-old living in Thornhill, Ontario. Craig noticed a newspaper article about Iqbal Masih's death. He gathered a group of his seventh-grade classmates, and together they formed the organization Free the Children. Today, Free the Children is the world's largest network of children helping other children. They accomplish this through education and youth leadership training in forty-five countries.[26]

Assessing Yourself

You may already know what issues you are passionate about and what type of organization you want to volunteer with. That is great. But for many people, the choice is not obvious. If you do not know, take some time to figure it out.

Quickie Quiz[1]

Check the box next to each statement that interests you. For each one you check, give yourself one point. If you are too young for some of these activities, that is ok. Just mark what interests you. Be honest with yourself and select only those things that you would really do. For example, if you like the idea of having a pet, but don't like cleaning up the messes they make, don't count it.

Animal Rights

☐ Rescue an injured animal.

☐ Get a pet dog and take care of it.

☐ Check to see whether products you use are tested on animals and avoid buying them.

☐ Protest or boycott companies that treat animals poorly.

Total: _____

Promoting Tolerance

☐ Create a voter guide that informs people in your community about the candidates for whom they will be voting, their voting records, and a complete explanation of issues at hand.

☐ Volunteer to be a Big Brother or Big Sister.

☐ Arrange a discussion group about issues of acceptance that concern you, such as gun control, abortion, homophobia, or racism.[2]

☐ Organize a "Mix-it-Up" day at school, where you eat lunch with someone you don't usually sit with.

Total: _____

Environmental Issues

☐ Measure your environmental footprint by calculating the amount of energy you create and waste.[3]

☐ Organize a neighborhood cleanup day and spruce up your favorite local park.

☐ Seek out places to buy organic and local produce when it is in season.

☐ Try walking, biking, or using public transportation more often.

Total: _____

Health Issues

☐ Volunteer at a free health clinic.

☐ Donate blood.

☐ Assemble personal health kits for people

with illnesses such as cancer. Try contacting the American Cancer Society to see if they can use this kind of help.

☐ Partner with not-for-profit health organizations. Volunteer to blog, raise money, or transcribe notes about important health issues.

Total:_____

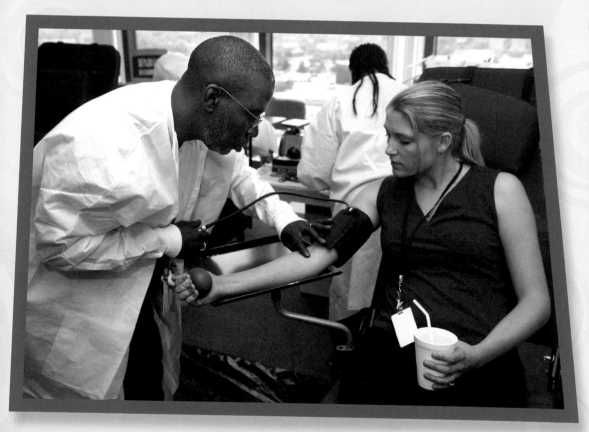

Giving blood is a great way to help others.

Rights & Liberties

- [ ] Establish an alternative newspaper.

- [ ] Study the Bill of Rights and organize a seminar to describe one that you see is being violated.

- [ ] Get your school involved in a program like First Amendment Schools, a national initiative to transform how schools teach and practice the rights and responsibilities of citizenship.

- [ ] Start a petition to address civil rights violations, such as Freedom of Speech.

Total: _____

Literacy

- [ ] Volunteer to read stories to children.

- [ ] Ask at your local library about English as Second Language training, and sign up for training and tutoring.

- [ ] Do you speak more than one language? If so, find an organization in your community that helps people who speak that language. Volunteer your services as a translator.

☐ Find an after-school program for kids who need tutors and volunteer to work with them.

Total:_____

Add It Up

Look at all your totals. Is there an area where you checked all four statements? Find the area with the highest total and rank it as #1, rank the second highest as #2, and the third as #3. If you are still unsure about what issue you would like to help with try the following exercise.

List five things about your community that really bug you.

1. _____

2. _____

3. _____

4. _____

5. _____

Is there a common theme? For example, are you annoyed by litter on the side of the road? If so, environmental activism may be the thing for you. Or, do you think that some of the courses in your school should be improved? If so, civil rights and liberties may be your thing. Or, pick the thing on your list that bugs you the most. Can you think of a way to improve the situation?

Two teen girls take part in a cleanup in Huntington Beach, California. Taking care of the environment may be a way you would like to volunteer.

Volunteering

Many community groups are looking for volunteers, and some ideas may not have occurred to you. Hospitals, libraries, and churches use volunteers for a great deal of their work and can use your help. But here are some volunteer opportunities that may not have crossed your mind.

- Day care centers, neighborhood watch organizations, and public schools

- Prisons, halfway houses, drug rehabilitation centers, fraternal organizations (such as the Lions Club), and civic clubs

- Retirement centers, homes for the elderly, Meals on Wheels, soup kitchens, food pantries, and shelters for battered women and children

- Museums, community theaters, and art galleries

- Community choirs, bands, and orchestras

- Local parks, recreation centers, sports teams, youth organizations, and after-school programs

- Historical restorations, monuments, battlefields, and national parks

What Is a Volunteer Worth?

The folks at the Independent Sector—a partnership of charities, foundations, corporations, and individuals—have calculated the dollar value of volunteer time. They have been doing this every year since 1980. In 2009, they calculated that the estimated dollar value of U.S. volunteer time was $20.85 per hour.

About 8.24 million young people ages 16 to 24 volunteered in 2008, over 441,000 more than in 2007. The volunteer rate for this group increased significantly from 20.8 percent in 2007 to 21.9 percent in 2008. The interest among young people in volunteering coincides with their reported increase in the belief that it is important to help people in need.[4]

Volunteering's Impact

As you decide what issues you would like to help with, here are some things to keep in mind.

- Change is often slow. It would be nice if your volunteering worked wonders overnight, but most likely, that is not going to happen. Still, it does not mean that you shouldn't take action. Your efforts at making this world the kind of place you think it should be counts for something.

If you love animals, you might consider volunteering at a shelter or advocating for animal rights.

Assessing Yourself

Just because you chose one opportunity doesn't mean you can't choose another. Different things will become important to you at various points in your life. You may start off serving food at a homeless shelter and discover that what you really want to do is improve the laws governing public assistance in your state.

- Remember that a lot of issues overlap. For example, promoting tolerance can mean a lot of things: tolerance of people with sexual differences, racial differences, or cultural differences.

- Sometimes the cause that interests you most may be one with which you have a personal relationship. For example, you may want to work for the American Cancer Society because you know someone who battled cancer. A cause that helps you and your family is a cause that can help everyone.

- Try to get your friends involved. It is always more fun to do things in a group, and your friends may have valuable ideas to share. Also, working toward a common goal can bring you even closer together.

- Let adults help you, but don't let them take over. You are the one who decides what you are passionate about and how you want to help. Remember, with persistence and patience you can make a difference.

Volunteering

A volunteer returns library books to the shelves. Libraries, hospitals, churches, and schools often depend on volunteers.

Assessing Yourself

Daniel Kent is one volunteer who took initiative and made a difference where he saw a need. Daniel is a computer guy. He has been interested in computers since he was four years old. But Daniel isn't just about the computers. He is a volunteer at his local library, where he teaches computer basics to anyone who is interested.

When he was in eighth grade, an older man who he had taught told Daniel how much he had enjoyed the class. The man told Daniel that he had been "talking with a friend at his retirement home who was wheelchair bound and had no transportation to the public library."[5] Daniel wanted to help the man's friend and started looking around for an organization that might go to the retirement home and give classes. He didn't find one, so he started his own and called it Senior Connects.

The mission of Senior Connects is to help seniors living by themselves gain affordable access to computers and the skills to use them. The organization also aims to create a national youth and senior citizen empowerment program that links older people with middle-school, high-school, and college students.

Daniel said, "Initially, one of the greatest obstacles we faced was the fact that many retirement homes lacked computers. So we soon got into the business of refurbishing computers."[6] With a group of friends, Daniel went looking for computer donations. They contacted libraries, schools, and local businesses. The group also borrowed computer manuals from the library and used them as a starting point to write curricula. They also made the machines senior friendly. For example, they enlarged the font display on each refurbished computer.

Senior Connects was completely youth driven. Daniel and his friends managed the group, elected board members, and even began to set themselves up as a nonprofit organization. But as that process began, Daniel and his group found out that minors cannot legally be responsible for certain things, such as large sums of money. So they found some adults with experience in youth empowerment and nonprofit organizations. They helped the group create a youth-adult board in which the students make up two-thirds of the board.

Daniel says that most of the adults work in the same areas as the student volunteers. The adults include a high school principal, information technology professionals, and lawyers. "I'm currently fascinated with education, computers, and law so it works well for me," Daniel said.[7] The adults are great at navigating all the paperwork, and though they have no binding vote, the adults do offer the young people their recommendations about what projects to take on next.

Daniel's idea has grown by leaps and bounds. He has gotten inquiries from San Jose, California; Atlanta, Georgia; Syracuse, New York; and Winnipeg, Canada. But teaching

Computer-savvy young people can help their elders become more familiar with technology.

senior citizens how to use computers is only the beginning. Computers are of little use to those who don't know how to use the Internet. Finding information online and using electronic communication, such as e-mail, are very important skills in today's world. Daniel has established NetLiteracy to spread Internet literacy in his home state of Indiana and beyond. One of Daniel's main objectives is to create a program that can be repeated in communities throughout the country.

Volunteering

Though change can be slow, Daniel has actually seen the positive results of his work:

> One of our first students, . . . Dr. Grinnan, had a number of grandchildren that he was unable to stay in contact with very frequently because they lived pretty far away. He was one of the first individuals who signed up and he was very enthusiastic. I guess enthusiasm is very contagious because we were all excited. [Now he and his grandchildren] correspond back and forth with each other. . . . It's just really awesome to not only help your community but also to make new friends with people who you might not ordinarily meet.[8]

Causes and Opportunities

There are many causes for which you can volunteer your time. Hopefully you have been able to decide on which causes you would most like to focus. Now, you should consider where you can find volunteer opportunities that support these causes.

Causes

The Prudential Spirit of Community Awards Program honors young people in middle school and high school for outstanding volunteer service. In 2005, this organization reported that of the 1,040 young people the program has honored, the most popular youth volunteer activity was helping or comforting sick or disabled people. The next most popular activities were aiding the disadvantaged, enhancing school or community resources, tutoring or mentoring young people, promoting health and safety, and reaching out to senior citizens.

In School

When you begin looking for volunteer opportunities, one of the first places to look is your school. Since you spend a lot of time at school, it is a natural place to start looking. You may even see some things around your school that need change. Also, some schools may offer the opportunity for students to participate in service learning, in which students volunteer in their communities then return to school and consider what they've learned from their experiences.

Palo Verde Middle School is the largest middle school in the Washington Elementary School District of Arizona. The school's population is constantly changing. There are students from many parts of the world: Vietnam, Mexico, Central America, and Africa. Rich Curtin, a seventh-grade history teacher at the school, says that twenty-three different languages

Percentage Distribution of Young People Honored by the Prudential Spirit of Community Awards Program[1]

Cause	Percentage
Comforting sick or disabled people	22.2
Helping disadvantaged people	20.2
Improving school or community resources	10.0
Teaching, tutoring, mentoring, literacy efforts	9.4
Reaching out to senior citizens	6.7
Spreading spirit of volunteerism	6.0
Promoting health and safety	5.6
Protecting the environment	4.7
Fighting substance abuse, violence, or crime	3.5
Addressing needs in other countries	3.4
Promoting tolerance or diversity	1.9
Providing disaster relief	1.8
Taking care of animals	1.6
Honoring servicemen and servicewomen	0.9
Helping in other ways	2.2

A recent survey showed that helping disabled or sick people was the most popular volunteer activity among teens.

Causes and Opportunities

are spoken at the school. But although they are from different cultures, everyone in the school learns about their rights and responsibilities as Americans and how to protect those rights.

Curtin says that being aware of First Amendment rights gives students and community members an outlet for their views and lets them participate actively and publicly in their community. They have launched *The Panther Press*, a school and community newspaper in which students and parents get to have their say. Curtin says:

> We have a student senate and student council
> and are exploring combining them by
> amending our school's constitution. The

Student senators from Palo Verde Middle School raise the American flag. All students at the middle school learn about their rights and responsibilities as U.S. citizens.

student senate (my pride and joy) has organized a clothing drive to benefit a local homeless shelter. The senate, with the school administration, sponsors "Adopt a Spot," a program designed to promote campus beautification. On January 31, five senators participated in the city of Phoenix's Youth Town Hall. They met in groups of high schoolers and middle schoolers to debate current issues affecting teens. The senators are now debating a bill to sponsor a prevention group called Teens Against Under-aged Drinking (TAU'd). And in April, they'll participate in our school's Diversity Day.[2]

It is not always easy to change something at your school. Doris Le was a senior at Vallejo High School in Vallejo City, California, when she led a group of her peers to protest the conditions in school restrooms. Le said: "Clogged toilets, missing stall doors, urine on the floor, invisible toilet paper, and non-existent soap—these are a few of the problems that plague the restrooms at my high school. The school and school district had turned a blind eye to the hygienically and legally justified demands of students to fix these problems for years."[3] The students believed that clean facilities were important to their education and health. Le filed an official complaint against the school for having unclean, unsafe, and unavailable bathrooms. She also circulated a

Causes and Opportunities

Teens help out with a 4-H toy drive. Organizations such as Boy Scouts, 4-H, and United Way may offer opportunities for you to start volunteering.

petition demanding that the school district hire enough custodians to keep bathrooms in compliance with the law. The school was not thrilled about the scandal, but Le was resolute. She said:

The school and school district were not happy to hear such an uproar about a situation they thought they had under control. They also did not appreciate the sudden probing questions from the press about mismanagement and incompetence. . . . But I stuck by my campaign because students deserve clean, working, accessible restrooms; it's the human thing and the legal thing.[4]

If you want to make a strong statement, one of the best things you can do is get your classmates involved. Chances are if you are seeing something wrong at your school, others are too. As one youth organizer puts it, "When you have five fingers alone, it doesn't deliver a blow as strong as if those five fingers were together."[5]

There are a number of organizations that can help you bring those five fingers together. For example, an organization called SoundOut can put you in touch with other students who are trying to initiate change within schools.

After School

Many after-school programs can help you get into volunteering, be it through Boy Scouts, Girl Scouts, 4-H, or United Way. You may also find opportunities to volunteer through a church, mosque, or synagogue. The trick is finding the organization that offers volunteer opportunities that best fit what you want to do. Here is a sampling of the kinds of things you could do after school.

Boy Scouts or Girl Scouts of America. Scouting can be a good way for you to find volunteer opportunities. Amrita and Shrutika Sankar used scouting as a way to pursue an issue that was very important to them. They wanted to help end the cycle of poverty in Kuthambakkam, a small village in Tamil Nadu, India. They used a Girl Scout Gold Award Project to make their vision a reality.

Amrita focused on improving the quality of education in the village by introducing new educational resources (such as books and computers), painting murals, and engaging the students with educational posters and special events to foster school spirit. Amrita said of her Gold Award Project, "I feel that the experience of planning your own project and carrying it through to completion builds self-confidence that can't be done through anything else. Knowing that you have made a difference through a huge self-engineered project is so rewarding, and you know that you have left a lasting impression in the community that you helped."[6]

For her project, Shrutika Sankar identified sponsors, gained support from village elders, and improved the school's building. She oversaw reconstruction and installation of new flooring, replastering, painting, construction of false ceilings and a partition, and replacement of doors and windows. She also helped build a network of nonprofit organizations to continue the work she started.

The sisters agree that Girl Scouts has affected them profoundly. Says Shrutika, "I have met some amazing women ranging from troop leaders to program presenters, women who have become role models. Women mentors, who care that I succeed, believe that I can make a difference and will help me get there."[7]

Religious groups. If you are part of a religious organization, you may find a like-minded group of people who are ready to organize. Or you may find there is a group

A boy scrapes paint off a house that his church group is helping to rebuild. Religious organizations often have volunteer programs.

already doing something that interests you. For example, the American Jewish World Service offers summer volunteer programs for students between the ages of sixteen and twenty-four. In the summer of 2007, one of the projects involved young people building a community center in a village outside of Siguatepeque, Honduras. Jennifer Netburn and Sarah Goodwin, two of the participants, wrote of their activities while in the country. Their letter home gives readers a sense of what it was like to be part of a religious group and volunteer abroad.

From VS Honduras—July 13, 2007

Dear family and friends,

Our shoes are layered with cement and clothes covered in dirt, our water bottles are scratched, and our group feels closer than ever, like family. Here we are approaching the trip's mid-point.

Saturday morning, Isaac kicked off our educational session. . . . With the use of both secular and Jewish readings we critically analyzed the costs and benefits of our being here in Honduras. Our conclusion was that it was of course beneficial for our group to be volunteering here, but we acknowledged potential issues this raises. We questioned whether or not we were taking jobs away from Hondurans, and we talked about why so many people of the community want to move to America, what that means to their lives and local economy. On the work site, we feel that we are slower than the Hondurans, we are certainly not construction workers and they could work faster without us.

We also acknowledged the huge benefits that we bring by being here, for us and the community. The town and store is getting great publicity as we are helping to build the first two-story building in the area. For the group we are gaining hands on experience and as we are witnessing inequality we know we will be better advocates for things like fair trade when we return home.

Reports from both work sites bring news of progress and promise. At the store site we are beginning to see real evidence of the second floor. On Tuesday, with everyone's help, we took 210 cinder blocks up to the roof with a most efficient technique, recently coined "the human block chain." Starting from one pile of blocks on the ground, we handed them off to each other, one by one, across the road, up a ramp, and onto the roof. Throughout the week the blocks have been, and will continue to be, laid to form walls.

Work at the school site is just as exciting . . . Josh, one of our group leaders, initiated a garden project in which 50 students planted corn and fruit vines in front of the new fence we have put up.

Another activity recently added to our weekly schedule is a physical education program for the students at the school. Once a week for two hours, we take three groups on to the soccer

field and lead activities such as tug-of-war, relay races and yoga. We were pleasantly surprised at the students' passion for yoga.

Also we have been fortunate enough to make several visits to the homes of different community members. . . . We look forward to continuing these interactions and discussions.

Love, your happy Honduran workers! Jennifer Netburn and Sarah Goodwin[8]

In 1999, Lyle Whiteman took a job with the Unitarian Universalist Church of Yakima, Washington. The job was to direct summer work camps for young people to learn about the social injustices that farmworkers face and design service projects in their communities.

Whiteman had heard there were migrant farmworkers camping by the Columbia River in central Washington state. But he and the teens weren't prepared for what they saw. There were no services of any kind: no clean water, no bathrooms, no garbage removal, and no medical care. Many of the workers had come to the United States illegally, so they were hiding. When the teens delivered a report to Governor Gary Locke, he announced that regulations for improved housing would be put into place.

Still, conditions were far from ideal. In 2001, Heather Robb volunteered in the migrant-farmworker community of Crewport, Washington. "Crewport did not appear the way

many of us had imagined it would. The fifty-eight small, flat-roofed houses were built in the 1940s at the urging of Eleanor Roosevelt, out of her concern for the growing migrant-farm worker population."[9] There weren't any churches or community buildings, just a quarter-mile of road in the middle of farmland.

Robb reports that as they got to know people, the poverty became more evident. She said:

> Looking at one of the houses in Crewport, you would never have known that the family living inside had been without [running] water for fourteen days. You would never have known that its inhabitants, young and old, rose from the places they slept, in beds or on the floor, not knowing whether they would have jobs that day. You would not have known that the children had watched their father get arrested and taken away by immigration authorities, not knowing whether they would ever see him again. You would not have known that the people in the houses lived in fear of their neighbors, of anyone who might turn them in, for nearly everyone here has at least one family member in the country illegally.[10]

In 2001, more than one hundred migrant children lived in Crewport. They had nowhere to play except the road, so when asked what their community most wanted, residents responded, a playground. Robb's group set about pulling weeds, digging, raking, shoveling, leveling a path, sawing, and building. She wrote:

> For three days my job was cutting wood with a
> hand-held saw, something I had never done
> before. When we weren't needed on the
> construction, we played with the children.
> There was always something to do. Bit by bit
> the playground grew—swings, monkey bars,
> lookout tower, paths. As it progressed, I could
> feel that unseen growth was occurring on
> many other levels, too: trust, a sense of
> community, and most of all, the changes in
> our own awareness of the world beyond what
> we had known.[11]

In Great Britain, a new government-backed global volunteering scheme gives young people from less advantaged backgrounds between the ages of eighteen and twenty-five the chance to live, work, and learn about life in poorer countries and make a difference in people's lives. As part of the program, which began in the summer of 2008, youth volunteers may spend ten weeks in a developing country working on local community development projects, such as environmental conservation or HIV/AIDS awareness. When they return home, they give presentations to inform their communities about global poverty and encourage their peers to help.

Volunteering

Volunteers built a wooden playground similar to this one for the children of migrant farmworkers in Crewport, Washington.

This project is made possible by the collaboration of the British government with Christian Aid, Islamic Relief, and British Universities North America Club.

American Red Cross. You probably already know about the American Red Cross, an organization that helps people in times of need with food, water, blood donations, and other necessities. But if you travel to the southeast corner of Michigan, you'll see another side of the organization. Young people in the Monroe County Chapter of the American Red Cross operate ROCK (Reaching Out and Caring with Kindness), a health awareness program that relies on peer education. ROCK volunteers learn about drug awareness and other

Supplies for those affected by Hurricane Katrina wait to be distributed by the Red Cross. The organization helps out all over the world in times of disaster.

pressing social issues in the community, and they train other youth. The trainees then go on to become part of the growing number of youth who are actively engaged in ROCK activities, where they have the opportunity to suggest, create, and support their own projects.

Volunteering

ROCK works with a mental health agency, training youth with developmental disabilities to become fully integrated into the adult working world. Using the American Red Cross Babysitting Program, ROCK has started a new project to train people with developmental disabilities so they can get jobs in the child-care industry. The teens taking the Red Cross babysitting course aren't talked down to because of their developmental disabilities; they are an active part of the team providing service to the community.

United Way. The United Way supports communities in their efforts to identify significant local issues, develop strategies, and locate the financial and human resources to address them. Checking with your local chapter is a good way to find volunteer opportunities. For example, how would you like to ride in an ambulance as an attendant? The Little Neck-Douglaston Community Ambulance Corps partnered with United Way to recruit Youth Corps volunteers. These youth volunteers may assist adults in an ambulance or by dispatching calls. Youth Corps attendants with the Little Neck-Douglaston Community Ambulance Corps get CPR and ambulance training for free. They learn about dealing with time-critical situations, community responsibility, and the medical field in general.

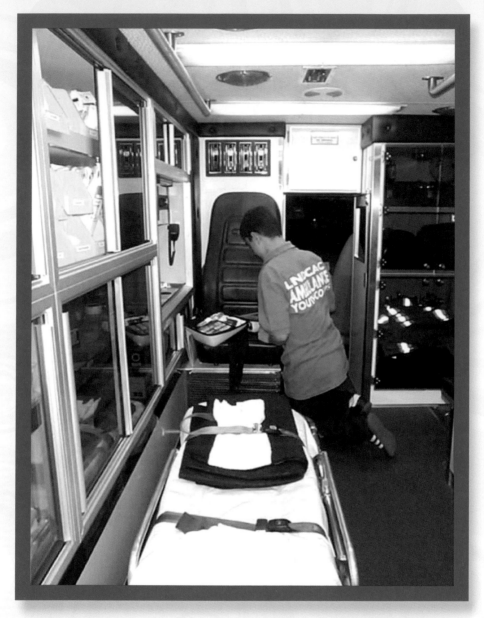

Justin Muller, a volunteer at the Little Neck-Douglaston Community Ambulance Corps, checks the contents of an emergency kit.

Volunteering

Justin Muller, one of the volunteers, found out about the corps through his mom. She had a friend with a son about Justin's age who really enjoyed volunteering there. Justin says:

> I really can't describe the feeling you get when you go on a call, it's different for everyone. I tend to feel a little exhilarated and a bit overexcited. At the same time, I am also rather nervous. You don't really need any special skills, just the desire, the ability to apply yourself to any situation that should arise, and most importantly, the willingness to learn. If you aren't willing to learn, volunteering at the Ambulance Corps is not for you.[12]

To choose from a large range of opportunities, visit United Way's national Web site. Enter your zip code or state, the groups you'd like to work with, the age group you are in, and the categories that most appeal to you to pinpoint the right opportunity for you.

Kids Care/Points of Light Foundation. Kids Care Clubs are groups of young people who work together to help people in their communities and around the world. With the support of the Points of Light Foundation and HandsOn Network, their goal is to get middle-school kids involved in things that matter to them. Each month, Kids Care Club posts different projects.

The kids in St. Mel School Kids Care Club in Woodland Hills, California, decided to collect dance clothing for a foundation in Bosnia-Herzegovina called Genesis Sarajevo. They also collected soccer gear for an operation in Honduras called Soccer for Life. Kids in the club put two big garbage pails, one labeled DANCE GEAR and the other SOCCER GEAR, outside the school's main office for one week. At the end of that week they had collected jerseys, shorts, socks, shin guards, cleats, balls, jackets, and a pair of goalie gloves from the soccer pail, and leotards, tights, dance shoes, costumes, pants, and lots of dance accessories from the dance pail. The kids packed up the donations and sent them off to start a new life with kids in other parts of the world who could use them.

The arts. Rick Lowe believes that art has an important place in a community. In 1993, Lowe, an artist himself, was living in the run-down Third Ward of Houston, Texas. He and six fellow artists—they called themselves "The Magnificent Seven"—started thinking about what they could do that would help their community. Lowe says he had a "eureka moment" driving down one of the ward's main streets looking at old, neglected houses. His idea was to rescue the homes and to create an environment where artists and the primarily African-American residents could live and work. He saw art as something that would help revitalize the neighborhood. He called his organization Project Row Houses (PRH). Now, more than ten years later, PRH includes twenty-two restored houses, thirteen units of low-income housing, an artist-initiated bike co-op, and an artist residency/gallery space. There is also an after-school arts education program. Fifty-five neighborhood children between the ages of five and thirteen attend classes that help them learn basic academic skills, such as organizing their

Murals created by young artists at the Revolving Museum in Lowell, Massachusetts. Many volunteers work in art programs.

Causes and Opportunities

materials, listening to directions, and completing their work. Kids get instruction in visual arts, music, Afro-Brazilian dance, drumming, gardening, ceramics, and homework tutorials.

The Revolving Museum in Lowell, Massachusetts, uses art to help kids tackle issues that affect them—things like drugs, violence, homelessness, divorce, cultural differences, race, and family. The museum began in Boston in 1984. Staff worked with kids who helped develop, install, and coordinate a baseball-themed public art project and community events. They transformed an abandoned baseball field so that the public could "come to bat" against the area's problems. The project was a huge success, so the museum expanded and continues to develop programs for youth volunteers.

In 1992, the museum sponsored a series of public art festivals called the Wonders of the World (WOW), including:

- Kid's Carnival (1992)—More than a thousand kids worked with artists to create interactive games, sculptural rides, billboard-sized murals, and performance art pieces.

- CRUMBS Company: Yeast of Eden (1999–2001)—A three-year project where kids built a full-scale "house of bread" to represent themselves.

- Stay-In-School SPOOL 500 (2005)—Kids built and raced more than five hundred art cars using spools as wheels (to honor Lowell, Massachusetts, home of the country's first textile mills) on a giant racetrack.

The Revolving Museum keeps revolving, developing programs and events designed to give young people a chance to be involved and discover how art can inspire personal and community pride.

"Do it yourself." Konstantine R. Buhler was eleven years old when he created a community service project called Always Ready Kids (ARK). "My first interest in disaster preparedness arose from the Columbine shootings in 1999, when I was 7 years old. . . . Then, in 2001 my Aunt Betsy survived the terrorist attack of September 11. She believes that the essential items she happened to have in her purse helped save her life."[13] After that, Konstantine became convinced that a way to help save lives in a time of crisis is through preparedness and that young people were the key to making sure that things get done.

ARK prepares kids for natural and man-made disasters by educating them on disaster preparedness and action through interactive lectures and by equipping them with safety packets. Safety packets include essential supplies that kids can use during a disaster, such as flashlights and batteries, whistles, and bandages. Corporations and volunteers support ARK, whose membership has grown from the United States to Europe. And they are still expanding, always eager to open new chapters. Their current campaign is called the Preparedness Promise, a nationwide effort to promote more preparedness-focused lifestyles. ARK members

Konstantine Buhler (in back) and a group of kids with emergency supply kits.

speak at events about what families and communities can do to prepare for emergencies. "We give them a pamphlet about how to make an emergency supply kit and encourage families to make the 'Preparedness Promise'; that is, set up an emergency supply kit at home."[14] Since the campaign was launched in 2007, 4,000 people have taken the Preparedness Promise, while over 15,000 people have participated in other ARK-run projects. In addition to helping thousands of people in communities across America and abroad, ARK has raised approximately twenty thousand dollars for disaster-relief efforts.

Buhler began ARK as a result of a Youth Venture grant and has continued to build the organization. Youth Venture is an organization that helps young people put their ideas into action. Youth leaders present their ideas and get guidance, mentoring, tools, and the support of a network of other young people who are similarly trying to make a change. The site also gives tips about refining ideas, writing an action plan, and getting funding. Buhler says that the people who work at Youth Venture are wonderful mentors and have supported him every step of the way.

There are many other organizations that can help you get your community service project rolling. Youthnoise is an excellent resource with practical information on fund-raising, letter writing, and public speaking. Their tool kits are authored by other youth volunteers.

Buhler says the most important thing for other kids to know about getting involved is that you are never too young to make a difference. Even if you start out small, in time, it could have a big impact. "With passion and energy, anyone can help change our world. You need to find an issue that you are passionate about and then carry out projects with energy and excitement. With hard work and perseverance, you will make a difference!"[15]

Youth Forums and Councils

Like the adults in your life, you benefit from participating in the policies, programs, and environments that affect you. Attending a youth conference is a way to do that. Youth conferences, such as the Students Commission in Canada or the National Youth Summit, bring together young people from different backgrounds and geographical locations to express their feelings about issues important to them and to talk with other youth and develop policies, strategies, and volunteer programs to improve their communities. These programs are based on the idea that youth can play a major role in helping to end world problems. Events such as these encourage team building, problem solving, and participation. Students also learn to work with others and take all the best ideas and turn them into a single strategy. Also, because government decision-makers often attend these conferences, attendees get direct contact with them, allowing them to exchange information and ideas that can benefit their communities.

If you've never been to a youth forum, it can be an interesting and exciting endeavor. For some of these conferences, you can't just go because you want to; someone—a teacher or community leader—must nominate you.

Also, it will probably be one of the biggest gatherings you have ever been to—as many as six hundred young people attended the World Youth Congress in Quebec in 2008.

Volunteering

Members of the Teen Advisory Panel in Mercer County, Kentucky. Youth forums, panels, and conferences give teens an opportunity to share ideas and plan activities.

Most likely, the conference won't take place in your hometown, so you'll be traveling to another city. Most youth forums last between five and seven days. Be prepared to work very hard—perhaps harder than you've ever worked on anything. But also prepare for some great personal satisfaction. Many of these conferences are also attended by adult policy makers who can make your ideas reality.

For example, the 2010 World Youth Conference, an initiative of the Mexican government, the United Nations, and other organizations, was formed to "bring together young people from the country and from all over the world in order to have a conversation and a proposal with Government representatives, legislators, and organisms of the civil society."[16] Government leaders were looking for unique solutions to problems of global importance.

At the Millennium Young People's Congress held in Hawaii in 1999, participants built a peace garden and, with the help of Peace Child International, established a program called Be the Change. This program provides funding to young people for small-scale community improvement projects in disadvantaged areas.

The "New Volunteer" Chapter 4

With new media and software becoming easier to access and use, you are able to share your thoughts and ideas with a large number of people via the Internet. Maybe you want to make a video and post it to YouTube. Maybe you write music and lyrics and broadcast them with streaming media.

New technology enables you to give in new ways. "Click-to-donate" sites let anyone with an Internet connection contribute to a charity with a simple mouse click.

Or maybe you or your friends are interested in the hardware and want to fix computers to keep or donate.

New technology lets you be a virtual volunteer, an "instant activist." Most often, this involves visiting a Web site and clicking to sign a petition, make a donation, or register to receive updates about a cause you care about. A lot of times, it may involve your sending an e-letter that has already been composed to a senator or congressperson. The only thing you may have to supply is your zip code so that the person who represents your area is contacted. A heads up: though many representatives do respond to electronic correspondence, writing and sending a letter to Congress via snail mail (the U.S. Post Office) is considered your best bet if you are looking for a response.

A "click-to-donate" site lets anyone with an Internet connection donate to a charity. Usually, the group running the site asks companies with similar interests to sponsor the cause; for example, a manufacturer of sports equipment might sponsor a health campaign. Every time someone visits the site and clicks "donate," the company agrees to pay a percentage of that donation. As Mikki Halpin writes, companies do this because "it's corporate philanthropy, which does exist (really!), but it's also a form of advertising."[1] There are a few things to keep in mind about these sites.

- Usually, you're only allowed one click per day. If you click one day at 4 P.M. and the next day at 2 P.M., your second click won't count because it hasn't been a full twenty-four hours since your last click. You can get around this by setting up an electronic alert or using a reminder program to let you know it is time to make your next donation.

- Avoid scams to get your private information. Don't give out personal information, such as your phone number, social security number, or full address.

Perhaps one of the earliest organizations to involve youth with digital media is the Global Kids' Digital Media Initiative. Founded in 1989, this independent not-for-profit organization provides opportunities for young people to become global and community leaders. Today, kids get to try interactive and experiential media—such as creating a space in the online virtual world Second Life, recording podcasts, or creating a digital movie. They use these tools to find new ways to learn about critical international and public policy issues as they become civically and globally involved.

In 2006, Global Kids ran a digital media essay contest for teens around the world to describe the various roles that digital media is playing in their lives. The MacArthur Foundation used the results to learn how they could better award grants to help digital media become a tool for learning. The really cool thing was that the awards ceremony took place in real life and online with the winners' avatars in Second Life.

More Interactive Web Stuff

Cool People Care is a site devoted to presenting you with ideas that are small, simple acts you can do every day to make the world a better place. The articles section of the site features "5 Minutes of Caring" in which the staff describe small ways you can make a difference. For example, you can take reusable bags to the grocery store, save pages from your used calendar, or donate to a charity of your choice. You can then click the "I Did It Button" on the site and log your comments.

VolunteerMatch, an nonprofit agency that matches people with volunteer opportunities, hosts a virtual volunteer section. The virtual section showcases opportunities that let you volunteer without having to be physically present at a specific location. That usually means volunteering using a computer, Internet connection, phone, and/or fax.

Video As a Tool

Today, video and digital cameras can make the world a better place. Seeing a problem, rather than just hearing about it, can really bring it home. Here are some things to consider:

- Video and still cameras keep getting cheaper—they're integrated into cell phones—and have many built-in features that make mastery of them easier. Software for video and still photo editing is readily available for computers.

There are new and novel ways to get around the traditional "gatekeepers" of media (the large TV networks or film distributors). Web sites such as Twitter allow users to make their own updates about what is going on around them. Non-governmental organizations (NGOs), live streaming, and video

A girl makes a video of her family. Many programs allow teens to share their experiences and advocate for their causes through the use of video.

messaging via cell phone are other ways to share information that is not being reported by major television news stations.

- Organizations such as Appalshop (United States), Chiapas Media Project (Mexico), and INSIST (Indonesia) make video more available to people around the globe.

Video is an important way for people to share their stories with others around the globe. There is a term for this trend: *video advocacy*. Sam Gregory of WITNESS, a human rights organization that uses video and other technologies to promote human rights, defines it as the process of using video as an essential tool for social justice and activism and as a way to bring about change.[2]

Puntos de Encuentro— "Common Ground"

"Using edutainment to promote women and young people's rights in Central America" is the slogan of a group in Nicaragua called *Puntos de Encuentro* (literally "Points of Contact" but meaning "Common Ground" or "Meeting Place"). The group started in the years after Nicaragua's civil war with the aim of promoting the rights and well-being of women and young people. Because these groups were so oppressed during the years of war, the founders felt they deserved special attention

in addressing postwar social problems, and they wanted to use the media to do it.

The group's first project was a newsletter called *La Boletina*. The newsletter caught on quickly because it was unlike any other: Political stories would run beside a reader's favorite recipe.

The group then turned to radio. Sixth Sense Radio *(Sexto Sentido Radio)* airs daily with call-in times for youth to talk about subjects important to them.

There is also a TV program of the same name. It is like *Friends* in Spanish. However, the show "takes on topics in sexual and reproductive health that are often considered taboo, personalizing them in stories that reflect the problems, decisions, triumphs, and challenges" of young Nicaraguans.[3]

After each show airs, *Puntos de Encuentro* uses their radio station to air programming on related issues. By doing this, they feel they reflect the complexity of real life and give young people a chance to spark a dialogue. As their executive director notes, "Minds don't open with one TV show. Real social changes are a long-term, messy process."[4]

Many other organizations also use new media, such as streaming video, blogging, and computer graphic presentations. Street-Level Youth Media in Chicago, Illinois, joins young people and media professionals in collaborations. Through this program, kids develop media literacy skills that let them evaluate and respond to the media, as well as add their voices to the mix. In addition to music videos and other multimedia productions, Street-Level Youth produce a TV show called *Live Wire* that airs on Chicago Access TV.

Books Not Bars is a project in California aimed at closing the state's youth prisons and replacing them with alternatives—such as regional rehabilitation centers and community-based programs. The program, sponsored by the Ella Baker Center for Human Rights, used video to bring together youth and adults to protest the growing trend of jailing increasingly younger offenders for increasingly longer sentences. Youth organizers in Books Not Bars say that the money spent on jailing young offenders takes away resources that could be spent on education, training, and jobs, thus undercutting "the opportunity to thrive." With the right support, young offenders can become productive members of society. Books Not Bars produced a video, a companion CD with lesson plans, and student handouts to help educate the public about their initiative.

There is also Just Think. Founded in 1995 as a response to the ever-increasing number of messages young people get from just about everywhere (television, radio, film, print media, electronic games, and the Internet), Just Think teaches young people media literacy skills so they can be better prepared to evaluate and create their own messages. It contains a section called "Links to Think" that provides useful links to media literacy organizations, youth film festivals, and general youth-oriented organizations online.

Photographic advocacy is based on the idea that images teach and influence change.

Volunteering

PhotoVoice

Closely related to video advocacy is photographic advocacy. PhotoVoice is an organization that is based on the belief that images teach and influence change and that the people who live in a community are best suited to create and define the images that shape their community. It uses a nine-step strategy that targets the audience, defines issues that matter to a community, and helps in recruiting participants. This way of participating in community change has some other important pieces. PhotoVoice projects are meant to be shared with everyone in the community, including policy makers and community leaders.

Youth participants for PhotoVoice projects have come from schools, church groups, vocational programs, clinics, and teen centers. For example, Big Brothers/Big Sisters of Middle Tennessee recently launched a PhotoVoice project for ten students in sixth through eighth grade who live in or around J.C. Napier Homes—one of the oldest public housing developments in Nashville. There, about 75 percent of the residents live below the poverty line. Most kids are bused to a middle school outside their neighborhood, and many know someone who is in jail. The Tennessee PhotoVoice project will train kids in documentary photography, as well as how to express their ideas about themselves and their lives through their pictures. One sixth-grade student took a photo of the iron bars in her neighborhood and called it "Barred In." Then her group talked about how there are so many bars in their

Digital Storytelling 101

As you can imagine, there are thousands of Web sites and books devoted to the mechanics of digital storytelling. When all is said and done, it boils down to four big steps.

1. Choose a Topic: Pick a subject, gather images to represent it, organize the information, and begin to think of the purpose of your story. Are you trying to inform, convince, provoke, question?

2. Make a Plan: Nail down the images and sounds you are going to use. Select the software for making your movie and then import your images and sounds to it. Modify the number and order of images and sounds.

3. Create Your Story: Make a final decision about your topic. Write your script, making sure that it provides your purpose or point of view. Use a microphone to record your script, then import that into your software program.

4. Show It Off: Share your digital story and get feedback. Teach someone else how to make a digital story. Give yourself a pat on the back. You did it![5]

neighborhood that it looks like a prison. They noted that sometimes the bars keep people out but other times they keep people in.

When the project is completed, all the volunteers' photos will be exhibited publicly at the Nashville Civic Design Center. The hope is that participants will develop a real skill and get a sense of empowerment by expressing their ideas to the wide audience of Nashville.

One of the hallmarks of PhotoVoice is that it emphasizes safety and the responsibilities that come with using a camera. Everyone who participates must sign a statement that describes the project's activities, risks, and potential benefits. Participants must also acknowledge that their contributions are voluntary. An important part of PhotoVoice is that it trains volunteers to use the cameras. After they take their photos, the group meets to discuss photos and identify common themes.

Digital Storytelling

If you have ever wanted to be the next Spike Lee or Steven Spielberg, digital storytelling may be for you. While there are many definitions of the craft, most of them revolve around the idea that you combine the art of telling stories with any combination of available multimedia tools (graphics, audio, video animation, etc.) and Web publishing. Typically, a digital story for the Web is a three- to five-minute mini-movie. Your story may be based on a real person's experience. The story can focus on a single important event in that person's life. Or it can be made up.

In either case, digital stories use the storyteller's own voice combined with images, music, and sound effects to grab the audience's attention and bring the teller's experience to life. Typically, a production is a collaborative process where some people provide production skills and others work on the story, making sure to bring out its most important aspects.

Digital stories help you preserve and share valuable experiences. They can capture a significant period in a person's life and show how that person and his or her community was affected. While digital stories may be entertaining, they also educate and inspire. Getting a true and honest picture of other people helps promote understanding, tolerance, and compassion.

Zines, E-Zines, and Self-Publishing

Zines (as in magazines) are self-published, not-for-profit materials, usually produced by one person or a small group of people. They are created "for the love of doing them, not to make a profit or a living."[6] Most zines are photocopied or printed from a computer, but production of them can range from handwritten or handmade booklets to professionally printed publications. Generally, zines are not printed in large quantities. They come in all shapes and sizes and cover all kinds of topics: fiction, reviews, political discussions, just about anything. E-zines are the online version, a place you can read what other young people have to say and where you can voice your opinion, too.

WireTap magazine is an example of an e-zine with a national focus. Its mission is to involve young people in informing each other about the issues that matter to them, such as education, juvenile justice, and drugs. In addition to training emerging journalists to create high-quality content, the e-zine gives youth a space for reflection and discussion where they can air their opinions and get ideas for action. *WireTap* attracts approximately eighty thousand readers.

ShoutOut is another e-zine by and for teens. This publication includes weekly articles about safe sex, body image, and youth leadership. Population Services International (PSI), an international nonprofit organization that designs and operates health-related social marketing programs in more than seventy nations around the world, supports the e-zine.

Teen Ink is a teen magazine, book series, and Web site devoted entirely to teenage writing and art. Your school might have it. *Teen Ink* offers teens the opportunity to publish creative work and opinions on all the issues affecting their lives—everything from love and family to smoking and community service. Since 1989, *Teen Ink* has published about twenty-five thousand creative works by young people. The Young Authors Foundation supports the Web site.

LA Youth is written by and for kids in the Los Angeles area, but it covers so much ground that youth anywhere will relate to it. There are firsthand accounts of teens' experiences with college stress, racial identity, homophobia, censorship, broken families, and many more topics. In addition, youth authors review books and CDs, sponsor essay contests, and provide a Letters to the Editor section. In addition to the e-zine, *LA Youth* is available in printed format. There are five full-time adult staff members who handle the business end of the magazine and about eighty teen writers. Even though you must live in the Los Angeles area to be a regular writer for *LA Youth,* you can always submit your ideas and log your opinions online.

Radio

Around the world, programs exist to give young people a chance to get to know how a radio station is run, learn what does what, and to broadcast live over the air and Internet. Youth radio can be defined as radio shows that have been

Members of the radio show *Teen Vibes* in Alexandria, Louisiana work in the studio. Their teen-focused talk show runs on Saturday mornings and afternoons.

conceived, developed, and produced by kids, and whose end result is not only programming, but youth learning, community development, creative expression, and social justice. Perhaps one of the best-known programs in the United States is Youth Radio. This is an after-school organization in which young people produce stories for local and national broadcast. The program runs in several cities: Los Angeles, Washington, D.C., San Francisco, and Atlanta.

Students in Missouri work in the control room at their high school's broadcasting studio. Programs exist all over the country to give teens the training and experience they need to let their voices and viewpoints be heard.

Volunteering

If there is an on-site program near you, you can get involved by filling out an application and requesting an interview. Selected students will attend after-school media classes twice a week for twelve weeks. There, they will learn basic media skills for the Web, video, music production, and radio by producing and hosting a weekly live show that airs every Friday from 7:00 to 9:00 P.M. called *Youth in Control*. Once students graduate from the introductory classes, they have the option to move on to more advanced training for another twelve weeks. At this point, classes specialize in a particular area of expertise; for example, engineering, music, video production, or news writing. After completing the coursework, students can intern at Youth Radio and eventually learn everything that they need to know about radio, from fund-raising and administration to organizing a newsroom.

Technical training is only half of the picture. When students intern at Youth Radio, they also take on other responsibilities. They help with the day-to-day running of the radio station, covering and distributing programs and working with adult producers. Sometimes adult producers will accompany youth reporters in the field—perhaps when interviewing a juvenile offender, interviewing a teacher, or covering a national event. Other times, an intern may mentor a peer. As they begin to gain experience, young people have opportunities to produce stories on commercial stations and high-volume Web sites. For example, on KQED-FM in northern California, Youth Radio produces a show that airs on the last Sunday of every month

Like these young activists, you can stand up for what you believe in.

at 4:30 P.M. Topics for the show range from odd occupations and dating to more serious issues, such as AIDS and smoking, all with the goal of informing and educating youth about issues that affect them. You can listen to this show on Youth Radio's Web radio station or on iTunes Radio under the Eclectic, Public, and Urban categories.

Another group that literally helps youth share their voice is Generation PRX. This group is part the Public Radio Exchange (PRX), a collection of public radio stations working together to maintain a library of public radio programming from which stations can choose content. Generation PRX is the part of the organization devoted to making youth-produced radio pieces public.

A Youth Radio project called Blunt Radio produces a weekly call-in talk show that airs Monday nights from 7:30 to 8:30 on WPMG in Portland, Maine. High-school age youth from the Portland area, both free and incarcerated, staff the show.

It's Your Turn

Now that you are familiar with some of the volunteering options out there, you have the tools to explore what you might want to do. Check out the list of organizations in the "For More Information" section and visit the Web sites listed. There are many national organizations that you can get involved with, but you should also look at local organizations that need your help as well. And, if you are not able to find an opportunity that appeals to you, you can also start your own service effort. Good luck with your volunteering!

If you're new to volunteering or can't quite figure out what you would like to do, check these resources. Their Web sites are loaded with information and should give you some ideas. (Just type the organzation's name into your browser's search engine.) Most are geared to young people or have a Youth section that will interest you.

Volunteer and Service Resources

Do Something
24-32 Union Square East, 4th Floor, New York, NY 10003
This resource has so much, it is mind-boggling. Check out the tabs at the top of the site to find causes you might be interested in, projects already started, and ideas for starting clubs.

Idealist.org
302 Fifth Avenue, 11th Floor, New York, NY 10001
Operated by Action Without Borders, Idealist.org offers nonprofit organizations the opportunity to post job openings, volunteer opportunities, events, internships, campaigns, and resources. Find volunteers who want to work with you by looking through the volunteer profiles. Check out the teens and kids section too.

TakingITGlobal

540 President Street, 3rd Floor, Brooklyn, New York 11215
This online community is aimed specifically at young people. Here, you can find inspiration, get information on opportunities in which you might like to be involved, and communicate with your peers.

VolunteerMatch

717 California Street, Second Floor, San Francisco, CA 94108
This nonprofit's mission is to help everyone find a great place to volunteer. In addition to the virtual volunteering section on its Web site, you can read volunteer stories and look for opportunities based on your zip code.

World Volunteer Web

World Volunteer Web, Communications Unit, External Relations Group, United Nations Volunteers, Postfach 260 111, D-53153 Bonn, Germany
Brought to you by the United Nations Volunteer Programme, this organization serves as a resource center for volunteering around the world. You can get news, learn about volunteer opportunities by country or by subject area, and look at photos of international volunteer efforts.

Youth Service America

1101 15th Street Northwest, Suite 200, Washington, D.C. 20005

One of the biggest and best-known resources in the United States, Youth Service America works in partnership with hundreds of organizations providing meaningful volunteer opportunities for kids ages five to twenty-five. Their Web site, along with SERVEnet, brings you the latest information about what is going on in youth volunteering service, award and grant possibilities, and notice of summits and meetings.

YouthNoise

901 Battery Street, Suite 308, San Francisco, CA 94111
It offers advice on how to get motivated, take action, and connect with others. On their Web site, read true stories of volunteers your age and check out the "clickerific" campaigns you can help.

Environment

Action for Nature

2269 Chestnut Street, #263, San Francisco, CA 94123
This organization encourages young people to take personal action and get involved with protecting the environment. Every year, the group gives out international Eco-Hero Awards to young people ages eight to sixteen for their environmental achievements. The site also provides suggestions about how you can act for nature and posts stories from kids, like you, who have done something for the environment.

Free the Planet!

218 D Street SE, Washington D.C. 20003

A network of students who are interested in environmental issues and want to take action. They network with each other and other environmental organizations, providing new opportunities and ideas for environmental activism.

Youth Media

ASNE High School Journalism Initiative

11690B Sunrise Valley Drive, Reston, VA 20191-1409

High School Journalism Initiative is sponsored by the American Society of Newspaper Editors in the hope of giving beginning journalists a boost and a strong understanding of First Amendment rights. On the Web site, you can read a weekly collection of stories written by students from all over the country, find links to high-school newspapers nationwide, or link to national newspapers with online youth sections.

Listen Up!

127 W. 26th Street, #1200, New York, NY 10001

If you are interested in making movies, this is a good place for you. Listen Up! is devoted to media and helps "young video producers and their allies" to develop the field of youth media and to make sure that youth voices are heard.

PEARL World Youth News

475 Riverside Drive #450, New York, NY 10115

This is an online international news service written, edited, and published by secondary-school students from around the world. The organization is inspired by the life and work of Daniel Pearl, the *Wall Street Journal* reporter who was murdered in Pakistan. PEARL aims to promote cross-cultural understanding by educating young people in the ethical principles and practices of professional journalism. Using secure and safe online forums, teenagers report on issues of interest to them. It maintains student editorial teams in Iran, Uzbekistan, Pakistan, and the United States.

Animals

American Society for the Prevention of Cruelty to Animals (ASPCA)

If you are interested in volunteering your time to helping abused or neglected animals and their habitats, check the kids' section of the ASPCA Web site. There you will find a link to Real Issues, which include suggestions for helping promote animal-friendly legislation, ten ideas for fighting animal cruelty, and instructions for how you can volunteer at animal shelters. If you find that your desire to help animals goes beyond volunteering, there is also a section on cool animal careers.

Student Animal Rights Alliance

P.O. Box 932, New York, NY 10013-0864

This youth-led organization supports and connects young animal advocates to build a strong and diverse youth movement for animals. The organization understands the unique positions youth hold in their schools and communities for speaking up for animals.

Tolerance, Human Rights

Advocates for Youth

2000 M Street, NW, Suite 750, Washington, D.C. 20036
Advocates for Youth helps young people make informed and responsible decisions about their reproductive and sexual health. It provides information, training, and strategic assistance to youth-serving organizations, policy makers, youth activists, and the media in the United States and the developing world.

Facing History and Ourselves—Be the Change: Upstanders for Human Rights

16 Hurd Road, Brookline, MA 02445-6919
This resource provides profiles of some young adults who stood up for human rights. At this Web site, check the "Student Spotlights" to read about some everyday heroes. Then learn how to nominate someone you know for recognition.

First Amendment Schools

Association for Supervision and Curriculum Development
1703 N. Beauregard Street, Alexandria, VA 22311
This program works with schools to ensure that primary- and secondary-school students learn and practice the rights and responsibilities of citizenship that frame civic life in the United States. By establishing First Amendment schools in every state, the program educates school leaders, teachers, school board members, attorneys, and most importantly, students about the meaning and significance of the First Amendment.

Make the Road by Walking Youth Power Project

301 Grove Street, Brooklyn, NY 11237
The Youth Power Project at Make the Road New York focuses on helping New York City kids ages fourteen to twenty-one to lead community change efforts on issues they are interested in, particularly in ensuring safe and secure schools, keeping rent affordable, and keeping neighborhoods safe. In the process, the kids develop leadership skills and learn how to work in groups and organize within their communities. The kids also work to set personal and academic goals. The group is made up of low-income and immigrant families. Though this group's efforts are restricted to New York, it is a good site to check out to see how organized youth can get things done.

National Youth Leadership Network

P.O. Box 5908, Bethesda, MD 20824

The National Youth Leadership Network (NYLN) is the first nonprofit organization to be run independently by young people with disabilities. It is made up of young leaders with disabilities from across the United States and its territories. It promotes leadership development, education, and advocacy for all youth with disabilities to attain their maximum, unique, personal potential.

Chapter Notes

Chapter 1. Who, Me?

1. Personal correspondence with Cameron Angeny, 2008.

2. Ibid.

3. Ibid.

4. Ibid.

5. "Youth Helping America," Corporation for National and Community Service in collaboration with the U.S. Census Bureau and the nonprofit coalition Independent Sector, November 2005, <http://www.worldvolunteerweb.org/fileadmin/docdb/pdf/2006/05_1130_LSA_YHA_study.pdf> (January 25, 2008).

6. "4-H Teens Are Hot Shot Entrepreneurs," *4-H Network News,* July 2006, <http://4-hnews.blogspot.com/2006_07_01_archive.html> (April 26, 2011).

7. Jimmy Greenfield, "Teed Off: Abercrombie & Fitch Is Back in the News, This Time With a Line of Controversial Shirts," *Chicago Tribune,* November 2, 2005, p 8.

8. Brandee J. Tescon, "'Girl-Cotters' Propose Girl-Power Tees to Abercrombie Execs," *MTV*, December 8, 2005, <http://www.mtv.com/news/articles/1517726/20051208/story.jhtml> (January 25, 2008).

9. Rosa Maria Teti, "Ecolenos: Alternative Energy Heating," *Ecología y Desarrollo* (Ecology and Development), August 24, 2001, <http://www.ecodes.org/documentos/exp_ecol.pdf> (April 26, 2011).

10. "Ryan's Story," *Ryan's Well Foundation*, n.d., <http://www.ryanswell.ca/about-us.aspx> (June 28, 2010).

11. Ruth Lister in Mary Langan, "Engendering Citizenship: The Notion of Social Citizenship," printed in Milton Keynes, England, n.d., <http://openlearn.open.ac.uk/mod/oucontent/view.php?id=399064&section=1.1> (June 5, 2010).

12. John Wilson and Marc Musick, "The Effects of Volunteering on the Volunteer," *Law and Contemporary Problems,* vol. 62, no. 4, 2000, p. 144.

13. Personal e-mail correspondence with Megan Nakahara, May 2008.

14. Terry Y. Lum and Elizabeth Lightfoot, "The Effects of Volunteering on the Physical and Mental Health of Older People," *Research on Aging,* vol. 27, no. 1, 2005, p. 49.

15. Personal e-mail correspondence with Kayi Lau, May 2008.

16. Personal e-mail with Aislynn Rodeghiero, June 2010.

17. Aislynn Rodeghiero in Peter Schworm, "Comfort to the Hungry and Lonely, Meal Fills Rising Need," *Boston Globe*, October 16, 2005, <http://www. boston.com/news/local/articles/2006/10/15/ comfort_to_the_hungry_and_lonely_meal_fills_ rising_need/> (June 30, 2010).

18. Personal interview with Aislynn Rodeghiero, June 2010.

19. John F. Kennedy, *Freedom of Communications: The Speeches, Remarks, Press Conferences and Statements of John F. Kennedy, August 1, Through November 7, 1960* (Washington, D.C.: U.S. Government Printing Press, 1961).

20. Personal correspondence with Imho Colins Edoze, June 2010.

21. Ibid.

22. Population Reference Bureau, *The World's Youth 2006: Data Sheet* (Washington, D.C., 2006), p. 6, <http://www.prb.org/pdf06/WorldsYouth2006 DataSheet.pdf> (July 2, 2010).

23. Personal interview with Imoh Colins Edoze, July 2010.

24. Ibid.

25. Ibid.

26. "History," *Free the Children,* 2010, <http://www. freethechildren.com/aboutus/history.php> (July 8, 2010).

Chapter 2. Assessing Yourself

1. Format adapted from Diane Lindsey Reeves, *Career Ideas for Kids Who Like Science* (New York: Checkmark Books), p. 18.

2. "Test Yourself for Hidden Bias," *Teaching Tolerance,* n.d., <http://www.tolerance.org/activity/test-yourself-hidden-bias> (October 27, 2010).

3. "How Big Is Your Ecological Footprint?" *Center for Sustainable Economy,* 2010, <http://www.myfoot print.org> (July 7, 2010).

4. "Value of Volunteer Time," *Independent Sector,* 2010, <http://independentsector.org/programs/ research/volunteer_time.html> (July 8, 2010).

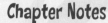

5. David Neilsen, "Do Something Spotlight: Daniel Kent and Senior Connects," *HowStuffWorks*, n.d., <http://money.howstuffworks.com/do-some-thing-spotlight-daniel-kent-senior-connects.htm> (June 22, 2010).

6. Personal correspondence with Daniel Kent, 2008.

7. Ibid.

8. Neilsen.

Chapter 3. Causes and Opportunites

1. Prudential Financial Inc., *The Prudential Spirit of Community Awards: A Ten-Year Snapshot of Youth Volunteerism* (Newark, N.J., 2005), <http://www.principals.org/Portals/0/Content/53443.doc> (June 22, 2010).

2. Personal correspondence with Rich Curtin, April 2008.

3. "2008 Youth Scholar - Doris Le, Vallejo High School, Vallejo, CA," *American Civil Liberties Union,* March 14, 2008, <http://www.aclu.org/organization-news-and-highlights/2008-youth-scholar-doris-le-vallejo-high-school-vallejo-ca> (July 2, 2010).

4. Ibid.

5. Emmanuel Tedder as quoted in Mikki Halpin, *It's Your World—If You Don't Like It, Change It: Activism for Teenagers* (New York: Simon Pulse, 2004), p. 61.

6. Lillian Willis, "GIRL SCOUTS: 11 Young Women Earn Gold Award," *Ridgefield Press Online*, June 28, 2007, <http://www.acorn-online.com/news/publish/ridgefield/19532.shtml> (March 7, 2008).

7. Ibid.

8. Jennifer Netburn and Sarah Goodwin, "Volunteer Summer 2007 Weekly Update Highlights," *American Jewish World Service*, July 13, 2007, <http://ajws.org/assets/uploaded_documents/07-13-07_vshonduras.pdf> (June 23, 2010).

9. Heather Robb, "Work Camp," *UUWorld*, September/October 2002, <http://www.uuworld.org/2002/05/feature2a.html> (March 7, 2008).

10. Ibid.

11. Ibid.

12. Personal correspondence with Justin Muller, 2008.

13. Personal correspondence with Konstatine Buhler, April 8, 2008.

14. Ibid.

15. Ibid.

16. "Frequently Asked Questions," *Youth2010.org*, n.d., <http://www.youth2010.org/site/content.php?page=faq&fid=0#cont> (June 25, 2010).

Chapter 4. The "New Volunteer"

1. Mikki Halpin, *It's Your World—If You Don't Like it, Change It: Activism for Teenagers* (New York: Simon Pulse, 2004), p. 10.

2. Sam Gregory, Gillain Caldwell, Ronit Avni, and Thomas Harding, eds., *Video for Change* (London: Pluto Press, 2005), xii.

3. "Programs," *Puntos de Encuentro*, n.d., <http://www.puntos.org.ni/english/programs.php> (March 17, 2008).

4. Gregory, p. 270.

5. Adapted from "Getting Started: A Step-By-Step Approach to Creating a Digital Story," *University of Houston: The Educational Uses of Digital Storytelling*, n.d., <http://digitalstorytelling.coe.uh.edu/getting_started.html> (September 27, 2010).

6. "FAQ: What Are Zines?" *Zine World: A Reader's Guide to the Underground Press*, 2008, <http://www.undergroundpress.org/faq/#whatarezines> (May 2, 2011).

Abaco Barb–A breed of horse that inhabits Turtle Bay Island in the Bahamas, which is thought to be descended from the Spanish horses who first traveled to the Americas in the 1400s.

activism–Efforts to change conditions in society.

bonded labor–A system in which a person is forced to work to pay off a debt.

boycott–A form of protest in which one refuses to use the services of or purchase products from a particular person or company who is perceived to be unjust.

citizenship–Membership in a community including a member's legal status, duties, and responsibilities.

click-to-donate site–A Web site that allows users to make donations to a charity with a mouse click; the money is given by a corporate sponsor.

empowerment–The right to make decisions for one's own life.

service learning–A system in which learning about an issue or problem is paired with volunteer work to address the problem.

zine–Self-published magazines or pamphlets, usually photocopied or printed from a computer. An e-zine is the online version of a zine.

Further Reading

Boles, Nicole Bouchard. *How to Be an Everyday Philanthropist: 289 No-Cost Ways to Live a Generous Life*. New York: Workman Publishing, 2009.

Egeland, Jan. *A Billion Lives: An Eyewitness Report From the Frontlines of Humanity*. New York: Simon & Schuster, 2008.

Gay, Kathlyn. *Volunteering: The Ultimate Teen Guide*. Lanham, Md.: Scarecrow Press, 2007.

Morley, David. *Healing Our World*. Markham, Ontario, Canada: Fitzhenry and Whiteside, 2007.

Nunn, Michelle, ed. *Be the Change! Change the World, Change Yourself*. Atlanta, Ga.: Hundreds of Heads Books, 2006.

SERVEnet (run by Youth Service America)
  <http://www.servenet.org>

VolunteerMatch
  <http://www.volunteermatch.org>

Volunteer Solutions (run by United Way)
  <http://volunteer.truist.com>

Index